Having Your Cake and Eating it Too:

Having Your Cake and Eating it Too:

Getting the Most Out of Your Flexible Spending Account (FSA)

Marion Williams; James Fleming

authorHOUSE

AuthorHouse™
1663 Liberty Drive
Bloomington, IN 47403
www.authorhouse.com
Phone: 1 (800) 839-8640

© 2018 Marion Williams; James Fleming. All rights reserved.

No part of this book may be reproduced, stored in a retrieval system, or transmitted by any means without the written permission of the author.

Published by AuthorHouse   02/20/2018

ISBN: 978-1-4969-3699-8 (sc)
ISBN: 978-1-4969-3700-1 (e)

Library of Congress Control Number: 2014916784

Print information available on the last page.

Any people depicted in stock imagery provided by Thinkstock are models, and such images are being used for illustrative purposes only.
Certain stock imagery © Thinkstock.

This book is printed on acid-free paper.

Because of the dynamic nature of the Internet, any web addresses or links contained in this book may have changed since publication and may no longer be valid. The views expressed in this work are solely those of the author and do not necessarily reflect the views of the publisher, and the publisher hereby disclaims any responsibility for them.

Disclaimer:

This book is designed to provide competent and reliable information regarding the subject matter covered. However, it is sold with the understanding that the author(s) and publisher are not engaged in rendering legal, financial, or other advice.

While the laws concerning the Flexible Spending Account (FSA) are centrally administered by the Internal Revenue Service (IRS), implementation of the rules is under the purview of Flexible Spending Account Administrators, third parties who interpret the IRS rules and regulations. The author(s) and publisher specifically disclaim any liability that is incurred from the use or application of the contents of this book.

Foreword

Since the recession began at the end of 2007, the average American family has been hit hard. Whether the issue is retirement accounts, jobs lost, levels of housing equity or the balance carried on credit cards, Americans have not fully recovered from the brunt of the financial crisis. In fact, while there is evidence that jobs have begun to recover, other measures of financial stability for families have remained stagnant. For example, the Federal Reserve Board has found that total net worth for families in the period Q2 2007 dropped significantly decreasing from 65.8 trillion to 49.4 trillion in Q1 2009. This is a significant drop in the net worth of households. Put another way, American families lost 25% or a quarter of every dollar of the funds in their retirement accounts. This loss, coupled with the losses in jobs, has made the situation facing all American families, except those in the highest income brackets, most daunting.

While this e-book will not be able to address all of the issues related to the loss of retirement savings or housing values, it does offer an opportunity for the average person the to free up some money that could be used to supplement or replace emergency funds, or add to retirement savings, or to just provide a way to deal with the unexpected expenses associated with raising children. Financial experts across the spectrum all recommend that individuals (and especially families) have three to 6 months of savings put away in a "rainy day" fund. Having these funds available provides individuals and families with a way to sail through life's unexpected challenges and most importantly prevents a reliance on credit cards. These experts agree that having an emergency fund is a critical component of financial security.

The reason that I wrote this book was to present information that if adopted, would detail specific tools and strategies that will allow the average person to:

- Minimize the burden of routine and unexpected medical costs;
- Allow the creation of an emergency fund, or free up funds to add to an emergency fund;
- Use a Flexible Spending Account (FSA) in legal ways that:

    → Increase the amount of take home pay in a paycheck!

→ Save up to 30% on income taxes, depending on tax bracket!
→ Acquire the goods and services but do it in ways that build your financial reserves!

The contents of this e-book are designed to be practical. The knowledge, skills and particular techniques suggested in this e-book have been used by wide variety of individuals – teachers, single mothers, recently married couples in their 20's – to improve their lives in ways that mattered to them. The results they received were noteworthy, because, in almost all of the cases, they were no major changes to their purchasing behavior. They received excellent results and you can as well. Keep reading for risk-free ways to lower you taxes, purchase items in a more efficient manner and use your money on things that truly matter to you.

Contents

Foreword vii
Introduction xi
    Background xiv
    Benefits of Flexible Spending Account (FSA) xvi
    Laws and Regulations governing FSAs xvii

How FSA Work 1
    Ways to Access Flexible Spending Accounts (FSA) 2
        Paying for goods and services upfront 2
        FSA Provided Debit Card 3
    Types of Flexible Spending Accounts (FSA) 4
        General Purpose FSA 5
        Limited Purpose FSA 6
    IRS Rules regarding what is an Eligible Expense 6
    General Divisions of Health Expenses 7
    Contribution Limits 8
    Why FSA Participation is Important 9

How You Can Benefit From FSA Participation 12
Tax Implications of FSAs 20
How to Use FSAs in Unconventional Ways to Generate Massive
    Benefits 22
    Refresher on the 3 Benefits of FSAs 22
    Creation of an Emergency Fund 23
    Use of FSA funds to contribute to Certificates of Deposit
        (CD) 24
    Creation of Vacation Accounts 25
    Creation of Investment Accounts 26
    Using FSA to fund Individual Retirement Accounts (IRA) 27
    Using FSAs to fund DRIPS 28

Conclusion 30

Appendices 33
    Appendix A: Unconventional Items that can be purchased with
        Flexible Spending Accounts (FSA) 34
    Appendix B: Best Practices for dealing with Flexible Spending
        Account (FSA) Administrators 35
    Appendix C: List of Qualifying Events 38

Introduction

Due to government policy, changes in technology, the erosion of pensions and the rising cost of the energy since the 1970s, it has been extremely difficult for the average American family to provide for their immediate needs, to say nothing of saving for retirement. Even prior to the 2007 recession, the national savings rate was already in negative territory.[1] Fuel costs, which prior to the recession were relatively stable, increased to astronomical levels, resulting in some families having to scrimp and save just to get to work. The issue in all of the situations mentioned above is that while costs and expenses have continued to increase at an astronomical rate, wage and salary levels since the 1970s have remained stagnant. The only reason that the increases in inflation have not completely wiped out some families (particularly those at the lower end of the socio-economic spectrum) is that women entered the workforce in record numbers.

These dramatic increases in prices combined with relatively stagnant wages have kept American families from experiencing financial security. As costs continue to rise, it will be even more difficult for lower and middle class families to find the extra money to save, invest or even take a well-earned vacation from time to time. The material in this e-book will assist families in finding these extra funds.

This e-book aims to accomplish several things. First, it aims to present knowledge, skills and tools that can assist the average American put aside some resources, enabling them to experience the relative financial security of the previous generation. Through the use of these knowledge and skills, it is hoped that American families can begin to understand certain things about how the financial system works and use this knowledge to make more informed choices as a result. Second, this e-book will explain the benefits of purchasing things (many of which are already routine purchases) on a pre-tax basis.

The beauty of purchasing things on a pre-tax basis is that is that it provides an immediate tax break. Using this method allows a person to receive a tax break as well as having additional funds to use in whatever way the person chooses. The best benefit of all is that you can use the FSA to

---

[1] It is estimated that prior to the 2007 Recession, the national savings rate at 4%.

get reimbursed. When you get reimbursed for the things you purchase, you get (1) the tax break; (2) the item or service you were going to purchase; (3) you get funds that can be used in anyway you choose! This three (3) step approach are what is going to free up resources and ensure that your family has the financial security it deserves.

The best way to appreciate the value that Flexible Spending Accounts (FSA) bring to the average American's life is to show what happens during a typical transaction and then to explain how FSAs provide tangible benefits in similar, yet more beneficial transaction. In the figure below, there is an example of a typical transaction that most people are familiar with:

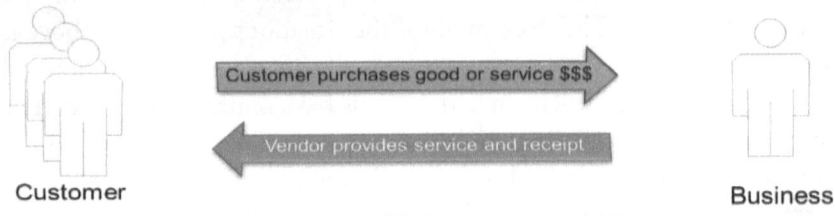

Figure 1: Typical Transaction

In the example above, the customer (or FSA participant as will be noted later) purchases a good or service, and the business, in turn, provides the good or service and gives the customer a receipt. There is a direct 1 to 1 relationship (i.e. Customer to Business and Business to Customer) for this transaction.

In contrast to the typical transaction, the Flexible Spending Account (FSA) Typical Transaction includes some additional elements. These elements, while adding some complexity, provide savvy individuals with the opportunities to access financial resources, grow their assets and substantially improve their quality of life. In the example below, the Typical Transaction elements are present, but have been augmented with FSA features:

Having Your Cake and Eating it Too:

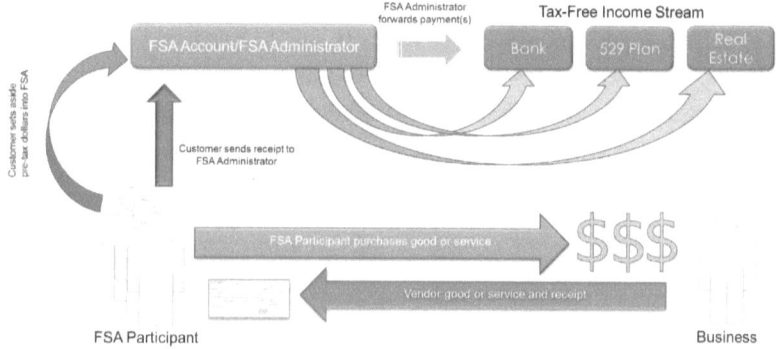

Figure 2: Typical FSA Transaction

In the example above, the FSA participant (this was included as the customer in the previous graphic) sets aside a predetermined amount of money (this is also known as the annual election) into the Flexible Spending Account (FSA). These funds are available on January 1st of the New Year or when a FSA participant experiences a status change.[2] Once a FSA Participant has set aside funds into their FSA, then they purchase medical goods or services as usual. Just as the typical transaction, FSA participants give dollars to a business for a good or service.

The primary difference now is that once a transaction has occurred, then the FSA Participant takes the receipt provides by the business and sends the receipt and a FSA Administrator provided form to the FSA Administrator. The FSA Administrator evaluates the form to determine if the expenses are legitimate.[3] Once found to be legitimate, the FSA Administrator releases the funds into the customer' hands either through check or direct deposit.

---

[2] A status change allows a person to make a change to their FSA election. For more details on status changes, see Appendix C for more details.

[3] The FSA Administrator decides if they expense is legitimate. If the expense is allowed or a person has a Letter of Medical Necessity, then the FSA Administrator releases the funds. If not, then the send a letter to the FSA participant explaining why the claim was denied.

On the diagram above, we show the FSA Administrator releasing tax-free funds into bank accounts, 529 Plans (College Savings Accounts) and Real Estate. Those examples were chosen to illustrate the concept, however the funds could have gone into Individual Retirement Accounts (IRA), to pay off credit card balances, or toward a dream vacation. The choice of what to do with the money is at your discretion.

Background

Flexible Spending Plans were initially conceived under presidential administration of Richard Nixon. President Nixon is most notably known for his foreign policy achievements. However on the domestic front, he was instrumental in a number of areas that relate to health care. Specifically, President Nixon made it a priority to deal with the high unemployment and rampant inflation that was plaguing the country during the late 1970s.

President Nixon wanted to encourage the market to address the exorbitant increases in cost of medical care as well as general economic pressures that were confronting the economy in response to inflation. In response to these twin threats, Nixon proposed the Health Maintenance Organization (HMO) as a way to rein in costs and inflation which was the principal factor responsible for increases in health costs during this period. The other major policy initiative was the institution of Flexible Spending Accounts (FSA), which use pre-tax dollars to pay for medical expenses.

Employers, fearing that cost pressures plaguing their bottom lines were threats to profitability, imposed annual deduction and co-insurance costs on their employee's health benefit plans. Employers also began to refuse to cover items that were previously covered under IRS regulations. Consequently, employees were now facing large out of pocket costs for the first time.

One of the realties facing employers and employees alike during the 1970's was rampant inflation – it made trying to save or purchase raw materials difficult. To address these difficulties, the IRS created the FSA to lessen the burden on employees who were reeling from these new costs. FSAs allowed the average American to pay for medical expenses that were previously covered under their normal insurance plan. This is especially beneficial since medical expenses are such that individuals will pay (and possibly incur debt) to take care of their immediate health needs. With

Having Your Cake and Eating it Too:

FSAs, those same expenses allow a person to purchase items they would have previously purchased, but do it in a manner that is advantaged by the IRS.

Aspects of the FSA program have been disliked by the employer and employee alike, there are elements that would indicate that Flexible Spending Accounts will be around for some time. According to the website, ZaneBenefits, an industry blog covering a number of insurance topics, employers and employees commonly have the following issues with the FSA program:

- Employees must specify in advance during the prior plan year how much money to take out of their pre-tax wages for their FSA (e.g. $100/month or $1,200/year). The employee loses 100% of any balance they do not spend in the subsequent plan year (or within the grace period following the plan year).
    → This effort may change with the recent IRS decision to allow employees to carryover up to $500.00 per year. Whether employers implement this new rule change, is largely at their discretion. Check with your FSA Administrator for details.

- Employers must make available to employees the full annual Health FSA amount (e.g. $1,200/year) on the first day of the plan year (e.g. January 1). This "Uniform Coverage Rule" means that an employee has access to the full annual FSA amount on January 1 even if an employee hasn't yet funded any of their payroll contribution. If an employee quits on January 2 after submitting and being reimbursed for a $1,800 claim, the employee does not have to repay such "pre-funded" FSA reimbursements after termination.[4]

---

[4] The IRS considers Flexible Spending Accounts (FSA) to be like insurance. That is the rationale behind letting employees access all of their funds on Jan 1 or whenever they join an organization. The negative side of the IRS ruling is that IF employees do not use all of their funds, THEN the employer gets to keep funds employees do not use within the plan year.

- FSAs encourage frivolous end-of-year "use it or lose it" spending, and don't reward consumers for wellness behavior by allowing them to save what they don't spend today for their future medical expenses.

With favorable tax treatment it becomes easier for the average American to pay for routine medical goods and services. This, in turn, aids the average American family in its efforts to be self-sufficient and provide the financial security that has been the hallmark of the American dream. The benefits outlined in this book explain how to use the favorable tax treatment offered by the IRS to enhance their quality of life and financial security for the average American family.

Benefits of Flexible Spending Account (FSA)

In companies across America, the Human Resource department is where most individuals get their information on pay and benefits. To their credit, most Human Resource departments distribute this information to the employee when they join the organization or during open enrollment. While the information they provide is often accurate, it does not always explain, in enough detail, how a person can truly profit from their benefits. Flexible Spending Accounts are wonderful tools that can allow an everyday person to save thousands of dollars, yet most employees don't sign up because they don't fully appreciate the benefits.

This e-book presents, in a useable form, information about how Flexible Spending Accounts (FSA) function and how the average American can use this knowledge to improve the quality of their life. There are several benefits that make FSAs ideal tools to enhance a person and their family's financial security. Most of these tools will be described in future sections of this e-book. Some of the benefits that Flexible Spending Accounts can offer include:

- *Increased take home pay*
- *Lower taxes*
    - → Lower taxes means there is a higher chance of getting a refund at the end of the year.

Having Your Cake and Eating it Too:

- *Additional funds that can be used to:*
    - → Save for retirement
    - → Pay for a child's college education
    - → Start or add to an emergency fund
    - → Take a well-deserved vacation

All of these benefits provide the average American with the tools to get the most of out of their paycheck. Using a Flexible Spending Account is like getting a raise! When an employee signs up (if they sign up at the beginning of the January) the funds are immediately made available. The employee can then make purchases prior to any funds being placed into their accounts from their paychecks.

For example, one of our clients learned that her daughter was going to need braces, in December. The client was a single mother raising a daughter in an expensive city. She did not know what to do. We advised her to use the FSA Debit MasterCard that was issued by her employer. She called the doctor, scheduled the appointment, and was able to pay for daughter's braces without any out of pocket expense. The funds on her FSA Debit card were paid to her Orthodontist. Since the expense occurred in January, she had not contributed one payment for 2014 plan year.

She was still able to access all of the funds in her Flexible Spending Account without spending a dime of her own money!!! This is just one of the ways proper use of a flexible spending account can provide funds to increase your quality of life.

Laws and Regulations governing FSAs

The Internal Revenue Service (IRS) is the part of the Federal Government responsible for oversight of Flexible Spending Accounts (FSA) program. The IRS also determines which, if any, medical expenses are eligible to be itemized on an individual's tax return.[5] The IRS produces and

---

[5] The IRS governs both the Medical Itemizations (which items can be itemized on an individual's tax return AND the Flexible Spending Account (FSA). It is possible for an individual to use up their FSA funds and then to itemize any other remaining medical expenses.

distributes rules and regulations related to the Flexible Spending Account program.

The most recent change to the Flexible Spending Account (FSA) program has been due to the passage of the Patient Protection and Affordable Care Act (PPACA). The PPACA, or Obamacare as it is colloquially called, represents the most significant overhaul of the health care system in the United States since the passage of Medicare and Medicaid in 1965. While these changes are large in scope, highly complex and impact numerous organizations, there are several major changes that impact employees participating in Flexible Spending Account (FSA):

- The PPACA has *lowered* the amount that employees may contribute to Flexible Spending Accounts (FSA) from $5,000 to $2,500.[6]
- There is now a requirement that drugs have to be prescribed (rather than being accessed over the counter) in order for them to be reimbursable.
- The PPACA has **increased** the amount of that an individual needs to itemize their medical expenses from 7.5% to 10% of their Adjusted Gross Income (AGI).

The PPACA has made several major changes that impact how the Internal Revenue Service (IRS) administers Flexible Spending Accounts (FSA). The rationale for these changes were made to enable the PPACA to be financially viable. The key point to remember is that while the health care overhaul is highly complex, the guidance provided in this e-book will provide the information needed to take advantage of FSAs and remain compliant with the new requirements.

---

[6] http://www.irs.gov/pub/irs-drop/n-12-40.pdf

How FSA Work

Flexible Spending Accounts (FSA) are administered by the Internal Revenue Service (IRS) and can be extremely complex programs for the layperson to understand. One of the primary benefits of this guide, is to provide the reader with the knowledge, tools and strategies needed to deal with the IRS requirements, while also providing greater financial security for themselves and their families. Since the IRS administers the program, it also determines what expenses are allowable and which expenses are not allowable under Federal law.[7]

FSAs are specific accounts established by an employer for their employees to purchase health care goods and services on a pre-tax basis. The value of these accounts is that when the employee purchases items using their FSA, they receive an immediate discount on their taxable income. This discount varies with an individual's tax bracket, but can be as much as 30% or .30 cents from every dollar earned. The other main benefit is that by enrolling in an FSA, the employee receives access to all of money immediately. That means that when an employee signs up (usually during open enrollment or when they start a new job) the money is immediately available BEFORE any money has been deducted from their account.

As an example, let's say Ann starts a new job and has been previously scheduled to get LASIK™ eye surgery. Since Ann signed up for an FSA when she started work, the funds are available for her to use, even though she has not received her first paycheck. The means that when Ann has her surgery, she can now submit receipts for costs associated with it.

This is truly beneficial, as normally there is a "switch over" cost associated with starting a new job (e.g. time between last paycheck and new job's paycheck, cost to move, etc.). With the flexibility of not having to spend money out of pocket for medical expenses, it lightens the burden of starting a new job. Another benefit is that normally 3rd party FSA administrators take 5 to 7 days to process claims. If a person's new job take two to 4 weeks to get a person paid, then that means, a person could use FSA to help them "over the hump" until they get paid.

---

[7] The IRS covers this information in the IRS Publication 969, "Health Savings Accounts and Other Tax-Favored Health Plans". This publication can be located on www.irs.gov.

For example, one of our clients started a new job and it was going to take 3 weeks to get a reimbursed. She has a Letter of Medical Necessity (LMN)[8] for therapeutic massage and needs some eyeglasses. She takes her FSA to a massage therapist and gets several massages for a total of $325.00. She then turns in her Letter of Medical Necessity (LMN) and gets the 3rd party FSA Administrator to send her a check for $325.00 which gives her some spending money prior to her receiving her first paycheck.

Ways to Access Flexible Spending Accounts (FSA)

Employers can choose between one of two (2) ways to allow their employees to access funds via their Flexible Spending Accounts (FSA). Both of these methods include the ability to access FSA funds on a pre-tax basis. These methods can also be combined at any time. This ability offers FSA participants a greater level of flexibility which, combined with the knowledge and skills in the e-book, allows people to get reimbursed on some expenses (e.g. doctor copay, prescription eyeglasses, etc.) while providing the ability to pay for more expensive goods and services without paying out of pocket (e.g. firmer mattress, C-pap machine, etc.).

The two methods that employees can access their FSA funds are:

- Pay for goods and services upfront have their funds reimbursed
- Use an FSA Administrator provided Debit Card

Paying for goods and services upfront

One of the primary ways that employees could access their FSA funds was through directly paying for goods and services and then submitting their eligible expenses submitted to a 3rd party FSA Administrator.[9] The FSA Administrator would receive the receipts and the required forms

---

[8] Letter of Medical Necessity (LMN) will be covered later in this book.

[9] FSA Administrators are companies hired by employers to oversee the Flexible Spending Account (FSA) programs. They receive receipts, ensure compliance with IRS Rules and Regulations, disburse checks and/or direct deposits to FSA participants, and perform other administrative functions.

and provide either a check to the FSA participant or if the receipts did not fulfill IRS requirements, they would send a letter and/or email out to the FSA participant informing them of what was missing.

The benefits outlined this e-book are really tied to this method of using the FSA for maximum benefit. Later in this guide, outlined are proven methods for taking FSA funds that are reimbursed and using them to fund an emergency fund, college savings accounts, or to take a vacation.

The key to getting reimbursed from the FSA Administrators is to comply with the IRS Rules and Regulations. It is also important to know whether your FSA is a general purpose FSA or a Limited FSA (Definitions for these terms will follow in upcoming sections). This will determine which expenses are eligible to be reimbursed. Just remember that some employers choose which expenses they deem eligible.

A noteworthy example would be the case of Condoms. Under the IRS Rules and Regulations, ordinarily items such as condoms and birth control pills would be eligible for reimbursement. Some employers such as the Catholic Church may decide that these particular items will not be reimbursed.

Since employers have some choice over which employee expenses will and will not be reimbursed, they can decide that some controversial expenses such as abortion will not be reimbursed. To avoid later complications, employees can read the Summary Plan Description (SPD) usually located on the FSA Administrator's website. Another way to address this issue is to call the FSA Administrator directly and ask whether specific expenses will be covered via their FSA plan.

FSA Provided Debit Card

The other way that employees can access their FSA funds is through a MasterCard or Visa Debit Card issued from their FSA Administrator. These cards allow employees a greater level of flexibility in paying for their medical expenses. These cards are designed to allow employees to access the funds in their FSA account without having to directly pay for their goods and services. The benefit of this approach is that some medical expenses (e.g. orthodontia, LASIK™) are very expensive and represent a great burden to the employee. If the employee can use their debit card to purchase this item, they can avoid a large out of pocket cost. This is especially important for lower and middle income employees.

In 2007, the IRS required that certain vendors maintain a card transaction system known as the Inventory Information Approval System (IIAS). The IIAS identifies FSA eligible items at the point of sale. Examples of such establishments include:

- Pharmacies
- Supermarkets
- Grocery Stores (Super Walmart, Target)
- Warehouse Clubs (such as COSTCO, Sam's Club, or BJ's)
- Mail Order merchants

The reason that some FSA Eligible expenses such as massage, may be initially declined is because the IIAS identifies them as being dual purpose (this definition will be explained in later sections). The facility where the good or service originates must be registered in the IIAS, otherwise eligible expenses will be declined. If an expense is initially declined, then the FSA Administrator will send, either by mail or e-mail, a letter to the FSA participant detailing why an expense was declined.

Once a FSA participant has received this letter, they have several options. First, they can follow the directions of the FSA Administrator. In which case, they will examine the reason for the expense being declined. In most instances, expenses are declined because they are either: (1) are not covered (i.e. an individual tries to purchase over the counter vitamins, without the Letter of Medical Necessity of a licensed Nutritionist); (2) do not include the proper documentation (e.g. participant submits receipts for therapeutic massage without a Letter of Medical Necessity); (3) the employer restricts some purchase beyond what the IRS does (i.e. FSA participant wants to get an abortion, but the employer has an objection on moral grounds (e.g. Catholic Church)).[10]

Types of Flexible Spending Accounts (FSA)

Part of the confusion surrounding Flexible Spending Accounts (FSA) arises because the IRS has designated numerous types of accounts as eligible

---

[10] Most of the time, the employer defaults to the medical expenses outlined by the IRS. It is always advisable to check with the FSA Administrator prior to large expenditures.

Having Your Cake and Eating it Too:

to be funded on a pre-tax basis. These accounts are similar to FSAs in that they allow employees to place funds into the accounts on a pre-tax basis, but differ in that they some of the things they cover. An example includes Dependent Care Accounts, which are used to pay for expenses associated with dependent care. Some employers offer pre-tax deductions for parking reimbursement. Each of these accounts creates similar types of benefits, however will only focus on FSAs.

For purposes of this e-book, we will discuss the two main types of FSAs. The two types of Flexible Spending Accounts (FSA) include:

- ✓ General Purpose FSA
- ✓ Limited Purpose FSA

General Purpose FSA

General purpose Flexible Spending Accounts (FSA) are general purpose pre-tax accounts that are used to by FSA participants to cover medical, dental and other medical expenses not paid for by insurance. Most common expenses that individuals use to pay out of FSA funds include deductibles, copayments, and other the counter medical devices (e.g. bandages, crutches, eye glass repair kits, etc.). The primary benefit of these plans is the fact that an employee avoids payroll taxes, Federal and State taxes, and is able to purchase items that normally would have purchased anyway. General Purpose FSAs or Health Care Flexible Spending Account (FSA) provide a simple way to access a tax break in addition to providing these other benefits:

- Placing more money in one's pocket
- For most individuals who elect to set aside the maximum FSA election, FSAs provide more than $5,000 in total benefits[11]
- Having access to resources to proactively plan for life's emergencies (e.g. kid breaks their leg, car breaks down, etc.)

---

[11] When the total amount of the benefits is taken into account, individuals can elect up to $2,500 per year and get reimbursed an additional $2,500. This is in addition to the 30% tax break. There are some additional funds that are deposited into a person's paycheck completely bypass payroll and other taxes.

Limited Purpose FSA

Limited Purpose FSA are similar in some respects to the General Purpose FSAs but differ in one key regard: The amount of items that can be purchases using a Limited Purpose FSA is extremely limited. In practical terms, this means that items that normally would be covered under a General Flexible Spending Account would not be covered. Examples of expenses that would *NOT* be covered would include:

- Hot Tubs
- Facials
- Mattress and Box springs
- Massages

While these items are normally covered under typical FSA arrangements, these items are not covered under the Limited Purpose FSA. Items that are covered under Limited Purpose FSA would like include more traditional types of medical expenses such as: co-pays; deductibles; prescription medication, etc. These easiest way to determine which type of account you have is to read the Summary Plan Description (SPD) or to directly contact the FSA Administrator.

IRS Rules regarding what is an Eligible Expense

The IRS has designated that general purpose Flexible Spending Accounts (FSA) can be used to pay for general health expenses. Specifically, they are, "… amounts paid for the diagnosis, cure, mitigation, treatment or prevention of disease or for the purpose of affecting any purpose or structure in the body."[12] In layman's terms, the IRS designates that FSAs cover the following:

- **Diagnosis:** The diagnosis of disease (e.g. Cat Scans, MRIs, Blood work, etc.) that occurs via medical exams would be covered by FSAs.
- **Cure:** The cure of disease (e.g. Chemotherapy, aspirin, antacid, etc.) would be covered by FSAs.

---

[12] This definition is from the Internal Revenue Service.

- **Mitigation:** Mitigation means to make less harsh or severe. Medical items or medicine used to mitigate a chronic health problem (e.g. prescription eyeglasses, orthopedic inserts, etc.) would be covered by FSAs.
- **Prevention:** Requires that there be a direct relationship between the treatment and drug being taken and the illness or disease being prevented.

General Divisions of Health Expenses

IRS rules and regulations divide medical expenses into three (3) major categories. These categories are important for the fact that they determine, along with other factors, whether an expense will require a Letter of Medical Necessity (LMN) from a licensed health care professional.

A letter of Medical Necessity is a letter (or sometimes a prescription) from a licensed health care professional that prescribes a course of action in the treatment of disease. With the Letter of Medical Necessity, it possible to use the FSA for expenses that normally would not be covered. Some examples of medical expenses that ordinarily would not be covered include: Gym Memberships; Yoga Studio fees; Personal Trainers; etc.

The 3 major categories that the IRS uses to classify medical expenses include:

- **Medical Only** – Expenses in this category would automatically be eligible for reimbursement from Flexible Spending Accounts. Examples include Acupuncture, Chiropractic services, and prescription medication.
- **Personal Use Only** – Expenses in this category are, for the most part, not eligible. The only exception to this rule, is where the doctor has provided a letter of medical necessity. An example would be use the use of herbs prescribed by a nutritionist. Normally these would not be covered, however if a person's physician refers a patient to a nutritionist and then the nutritionist prescribes herbs to address health issues, then the expense would be allowable.
- **Dual Purpose** – Expenses in this category can be used in treatment of a health issue and can be used for general health and wellbeing. A prominent example of this would be the use of Massage. Massage

can be used to create feelings of wellbeing, just as it can be used to increase circulation, improve symptoms of depression, among other clinically documented benefits. For this reason, the IRS requires a Letter of Medical Necessity to document that Massage is being used for a medicinal purpose.

Contribution Limits

The Patient Protection and Affordable Care Act (PPACA) is a legendary piece of legislation that has made a number of changes to the healthcare system in general and in particular to Flexible Spending Accounts (FSAs). One of the more noteworthy changes concerns the amount of money that can be set aside by employees into pre-tax accounts. These amounts are established annually by the IRS. The PPACA has lowered the limits that individuals can legally set aside to pay for medical expenses, while simultaneously increasing the percentage threshold that must be met in order to itemize medical expenses on an individual's tax return.

The individual threshold for an individual to itemize taxes on their individual return **increased** from 7.5% to 10% of their Adjusted Gross Income (AGI). This means that it is going to be very difficult for an individual to meet the requirement going forward. Given the new limits, most individuals will simply not have the amount of medical expenses needed to qualify under the new limits. To illustrate, let's say an individual makes a salary of $50,000 per year. Under the old rules, an individual tax payer making $50,000 per year could begin to itemize once his medical expenses exceeded $3,750.00 (7.5%). With the new rules in place, this same tax payer would have to incur $5,000 (10%) in medical expenses before he could begin to itemize any medical expenses.

The full long term impact of these changes will not be known for some time, however in the short-term, there will be some discernable impacts. The short-term impacts include the following:

- *Increases in the adoption of Flexible Spending Accounts* - One of the many benefits of FSAs is that they allow a person to lower their taxable income, but retain the purchasing power of their money.
- *Individuals, not in the know, will put off some medical expenses –* While medical care is an essential need there are documented

instances that show when individual medical costs increase past some threshold, individuals respond by restricting care. This effect is particularly noticeable after the employment level increases after a recession.

- ***The value proposition for the FSA will increase*** – Since the thresholds at which an individual can itemize medication expenses has increased, the value proposition offered by FSAs increase in two ways. First, the ability to access funds in a pre-tax manner means that it is easier to get medical goods and services. Second, because FSA lower out of pocket costs, particularly for expensive medical items (e.g. orthodontic work), FSAs can allow people to access funds in ways that limit out of pocket expenses.

The amount of dollars that employees can be set aside into pre-tax accounts is set annually by the IRS. The most recent change in the amount that the IRS designated can be set aside to fund Flexible Spending Accounts for 2013 is $2,500. As a result of the passage of the Patient Protection and Affordable Care Act (PPACA), the IRS lowered the amount that can be set aside by employees from $5,000 to $2,500.

Section 9003 of the Affordable Care Act established a new uniform standard for medical expenses. This new standard states that over the counter (OTC) medication can only be reimbursed from Flexible Spending Accounts (FSA) is they have a doctor's prescription. Insulin is the only exception to this rule.

Why FSA Participation is Important

As American society has experienced numerous shocks, such as the Great Recession, there have been a number of changes which have made it more challenging to save, invest, and have a measure of financial security. Whether these changes result from price inflation, or the shift away from pensions, or technological change, the result is same: Americans do not possess the financial security their parent's generation did. While correcting these ills is beyond the scope of this e-book, this e-book does provide access to knowledge and skills that can be used to create some measure of financial security. Taking advantage of Flexible Spending Accounts (FSA) allows the average American to take advantage of pre-tax purchasing, while simultaneously lowering their taxable income. Through participating in a Flexible Spending Account pre-tax basis, it is possible to:

- Lower taxable income, potentially allowing you to get a bigger refund
- Acquire the goods and services you were going to purchase anyway
- Obtain financial security for yourself and your family

The major reason that most people do not participate in Flexible Spending Accounts (FSAs) at work is due to a lack of understanding of the benefits. This lack of understanding is preventing the average American from acquiring the means financial security for themselves and their families. The table listed below will help to illustrate the benefits of FSA participation.

	Single Person		Working Couple		Family Person (non-working spouse)	
	Without FSA	With FSA	Without FSA	With FSA	Without FSA	With FSA
Total Monthly Pay	$2,500	$2,500	$4,100	$4,100	$3,250	$3,250
Less Non-Taxable Benefits						
Medical / Dental Expenses	$0	$50	$0	$150	$0	$250
Child Care Expenses	$0	$0	$0	$400	$0	$0
Total Pay Subject to Tax	$2,500	$2,450	$4,100	$3,550	$3,250	$3,000
Less Deductions						
Federal & State Taxes*	$700	$686	$1,148	$994	$910	$840
Social Security Tax	$191	$187	$88	$76	$70	$64
After Tax Income	$1,609	$1,577	$2,864	$2,480	$2,270	$2,096
After Tax Expenses						
Medical / Dental Expenses	$50	$0	$150	$0	$250	$0
Child Care Expenses	$0	$0	$400	$0	$0	$0
Spendable Income	$1,559	$1,577	$2,314	$2,480	$2,020	$2,096
Annual Increase in Take Home Pay		$216		$1,992		$912

Table 1: Illustrating benefits of FSA Participation

Table 1 in the table above, details three (3) main scenarios: a single person; a working couple[13] and family person with a non-working spouse. In each of these scenarios mentioned above, a comparison of monthly pay is made. This comparison highlights the scenarios of participating in a FSA along with the impact of not participating. The following scenarios illustrate the benefits of participating in FSAs, both in terms of taxes and in terms of increases in take home pay:

---

[13] For purposes of this illustration, this takes in account a working heterosexual couple. The IRS is currently in the process of drafting rules and regulations governing how same sex couples will be treated for income tax purposes.

- In the case of a single person earning $2,500 per month while participating in a FSA, this individual pays less Social Security and Federal and State Taxes. While at the same time, this individual actually takes home an **additional $18 per month** or **$216 increase in pay over the year.**
- In the case of a working couple earning $4,100 per month while participating in an FSA, these individuals pay substantially less taxes ($1,236 vs. $1,070). On an annual basis, these individuals will take home an **additional $166 per month** or **$1,992 increase in pay over the year.**
- In the case of a family person with a non-working spouse, earning $3,250 while participating in an FSA, this scenario yields less in taxes ($980 vs. $904). On the other hand, this individual will take home an **additional $76 per month** or **$912 increase in pay over the year.**

The three (3) scenarios detailed above show how that by participating in Flexible Spending Accounts (FSA), individuals are able to lower their taxable income, increase take home pay and increase their financial security. In all of the examples listed above there is one overarching fact: EVERY ONE OF THE INDIVIDUALS INVOLVED PUCHCHASED THE EXACT SAME ITEMS. THE ONLY DIFFERENCE WAS THAT SOME INDIVIDUALS DID SO USING A FLEXBLE SPENDING ACCOUNTS (FSA).

How You Can Benefit From FSA Participation

As has been demonstrated in the previous section, participating in an FSA can provide a level of benefits that is not readily available to the average American. These salaries used in the previous demonstration are salaries earned by the average American. In the above illustration, the salaries used to calculate the benefits received do not exceed $50,000, which according the Federal estimates only slightly exceeds the median family income of $42,000.

To further drive home the point of value of FSA participation, it is essential to explore case studies illustrating how participating in FSAs can impact individuals at different levels of the income distribution. In this section we examine the lives of several Americans at different income levels to see how FSAs can assist them at each stage. Presented are the case studies of 4 individuals. These individuals have all taken advantage of the Flexible Spending Accounts, yet they are at different points in their lives. Their situations are studied to understand how FSAs can assist a person or family through a wide spectrum of income. FSA expenses are highlighted in blue and tallied up to demonstrate the savings attributable to FSA.

Case Study #1 – Amanda

Amanda is 23 years old and just finished college with an undergraduate degree in Accounting. Amanda's top grades and 2 internships have led her to an entry level job as a Staff Accountant with a medium sized employer in the Midwest. The job comes with a salary of $40,000 a year and full benefits to include a Flexible Spending Account (FSA). Amanda signs up immediately and places $1,000 aside for medical expenses. Her employer issues her a FSA MasterCard Debit Card to pay for her medical expenses.

Over the next year, Amanda incurs the following healthcare expenses:

- Prescription Eyeglasses/contacts $250.00
- Eye Exam $20.00
- Doctor Copay (4 times per year @ $20 per visit) $80.00
- Orthodontist $850.00

Given the above scenario, it is easy to see that Amanda has more expenses than she has elected to set aside (e.g. $1,200 vs. $1,000). While the FSA does not allow participants to change the amount an individual sets aside (this is known as their annual election), in their benefit year[14], it is possible under certain conditions.

Since Amanda was able to take advantage of the information contained within this guide, she was able to use a combination of paying out of pocket for some expenses (e.g. Eye Exam, Doctor's Copay, etc.) while using the FSA Debit MasterCard for her largest out of pocket expense the orthodontist).

Amanda realized the following benefits:

- Lower Federal, Social Security, State, and Payroll taxes
- No **out of pocket costs** for her most costly medical expense (e.g. Orthodontist)[15]
- A reimbursement check for $150.00, that she can use for a vacation, retirement savings or on anything she wants.

---

[14] It is possible in some instances to change the amount of money an employee sets aside during the year. This is known as a "Qualifying Event". Typical Qualifying Events include marriage, divorce, birth of a child, etc. A more comprehensive list is included in the appendices of this guide.

[15] In this example, Amanda will not get all of her money reimbursed since she spent $850.00 on Orthodontist bills. However, she will get $150.00 back that she can use in manner she deems fit.

Case Study #2 – Edward

Edward is 30 years old and married. He has 2 girls ages 5 and 7, and has just been promoted to a supervisory position. The new job carries increased job responsibilities with a nice increase in pay to $60,000 per year. Based on the information in this guide, Edward has decided to place $500.00 per year of FSA funds for each of the girls (along with other after tax funds) into his state's college savings plan for his children, thereby receiving additional taxes breaks.[16] Edward has wisely set aside the maximum amount into his Flexible Spending Account (FSA) of $2,500.00. While Edward and his wife have certain expenses that they know that they will have, Edward's daughter, unexpectedly fell out a tree and breaks her leg.

Edward has the following medical expenses:

- Emergency room visit for his daughter $75.00
    - Medical Costs for daughter's broken leg (physical therapy, medication, co-pay, etc.) $1,200.00

- Co pays, prescription medication, and family planning supplies $300.00
- Firmer Mattress to help with lower back pain. $1,000
- Daughter's visit to speech pathologist $535

While Edward's medical expenses were substantially more than his annual election ($3,185.00 vs. $2,500.00), he is able to realize a number of great benefits that create value for him and this family.

These benefits include:

- The ability to respond to a family emergency (i.e. his daughter's broken leg) without undue hardship

---

[16] Most states grant a tax break up to certain limits for individuals to contribute to the state's college savings plan. See your tax professional for details.

- An extra **$267.00 or $3,200 per year** in placed into Edward's paycheck!!!
- Lower Federal, Social Security, State, and Payroll taxes
- Contributions to his daughter's college education through his state's 529 plan.
    - Lower state taxes as a result of his contribution to the plan
- Purchasing a mattress, an expense that ordinarily would not be covered, with FSA funds
- Reimbursement check for $700.00, which can be used to fund Edward's daughters' college education

Case Study 3 - Juan

Juan is 42 years old and works as a manager for a software development company. Between base salary and bonuses he makes approximately $80,000 per year. Juan has recently been diagnosed with diabetes, high blood pressure, and high cholesterol. Realizing that Juan needs to improve his health, Juan enrolls in his company's Flexible Spending Account (FSA). Juan enthusiastically enrolls in the FSA with the maximum election of $2,500 per year. Once Juan learns of the information in this guide, he uses this information to take full advantage of benefits of FSA. Juan's doctor has recommended that he engage in physical exercise and take medication for his Type II diabetes, high blood pressure and high cholesterol. This guide informs Juan that he take some advantage of some these things to work on all of his medical issues. Juan learns the following:

- The practice of Yoga has documented mental and physical benefits that can assist with his multiple diagnoses of diabetes, high blood pressure and high cholesterol. Juan gets a Letter of Medical Necessity (LMN) and pays for a yearly membership at a yoga studio using FSA funds.
- Diabetics often have issues with circulation in their limbs. Without adequate circulation they are a greater risk of limb amputation.

- Juan learns this information from his physician and learns that therapeutic massage can aid in circulation, among other health benefits. Juan gets a Letter of Medical Necessity (LMN) from his doctor and commits to get a therapeutic massage on a regular basis.
- Another major issue with Type II Diabetics is the tendency of blood sugar to remain high over time. Acupuncture has been demonstrated to lower blood sugar over time. Juan commits to purchasing a weekly session with his acupuncturist, with an emphasis on lowering his A1C.[17] Acupuncture does not require a Letter of Medical Necessity (LMN), so Juan can just pay for those funds directly either through a Debit card or directly out of pocket and be reimbursed.

With the information from the previous section in mind, Juan had incurred the following medical expenses:

- Yoga Studio Membership $800.00
- Monthly therapeutic massages $1,200.00 per year (1 massage per month @ $100.00)
- Acupuncture treatments $300.00
- Medication $360.00 (Diabetes, High Blood Pressure and High Cholesterol)[18]

All of the medical expenses that Juan incurred, were related to this recently diagnosed diabetes and related health issues. All of the medical interventions adopted by Juan possess the quality of medical treatments that aid the treatment of diabetes and its associated complications, while at the same time providing ways for Juan to experience lower medical costs and favorable tax treatment.

In Juan's particular circumstance, his salary of $80,000 places him in the 25% tax bracket. Juan differs from the previous listed examples, in

---

[17] A1C is a measure of blood sugar control over a period of 90-120 days depending on the test.

[18] The amounts listed for medication are for the applicable co-pays associated with these medications. If Juan had to pay the full amount (without insurance) for these medications, the cost would have been substantially higher.

Having Your Cake and Eating it Too:

that his income, ordinarily makes it extremely difficult to itemize things that will allow him to receive a refund check at tax time. Flexible Spending Accounts (FSAs) particularly make sense for his situation – it is one the few ways that middle class Americans can lower their taxes without extensive deductions. The result is that Juan can move into a lower tax bracket, save money and create options for him to have more take home pay.

Juan realizes the following benefits:

- Juan saves 25% of every dollar he earns and places into a FSA
    - Greater likelihood of getting a tax refund at the end of the year

- Greater take home pay
- Being able to purchase goods and services that have been proven to bring his diabetes under control, without undue financial hardship
- Freeing up resources to:
    - Go on well-deserved vacation
    - Add to an emergency fund
    - Add funds to a IRA, Brokerage Account, or Whole Life Insurance policy

<u>Case Study 4 – Michelle</u>

Michelle is 55 years old and lives with her 65 year old husband. She works as a middle manager with the Federal Government, and is trying to manage the medications that she and her husband consume on a daily basis. Despite the fact that she and her husband make exceptional income[19] ($100,000 and $75,000 respectively), she often ends up having to pay income tax and battle the high price of prescription medication. Once she learns the material in this book, she finds some excellent methods for reducing her taxable income, getting some assistance with paying for less of her medical

---

[19] For purposes of this illustration, Michelle and her husband file separate tax returns.

expenses with less money out of pocket, and putting some more money into her paycheck.

Due to the high levels of income that Michelle and her husband take home, she is in a unique situation. While the prescription costs that she and her husband are substantial, those costs do not rise to the level whereby they can begin to itemize their expenses.[20] The beauty of the Flexible Spending Account is that provides a great deal of flexibility. It allows an individual to lower their taxable income through pre-tax deductions and it lowers the Adjusted Gross Income of an individual, as it makes the 10% medical thresholds easier to meet.

Michelle currently takes medication for rheumatoid arthritis, diabetes, osteoporosis, and a host of other medical maladies. Even with her excellent medical insurance, it is still quite a financial burden. To meet the IRS threshold at her income level, Michelle is required to reach a minimum of $10,000 in expenses before she can begin to claim deductions for these expenses on her tax return. This means that she cannot itemize her medical expenses until she reaches $10,001 dollars.

Michelle and her husband have the following medical expenses:

- Prescription drug costs $1,300.00
- Occasional overnight travel costs for drug therapy $1,500.00 (these trips are in support of her spouse)
- Chiropractic visits (these are mostly co-pays, as most of the costs for chiropractic visits are covered by insurance) $480.00

There is no doubt that Michelle and her husband can benefit greatly from the election of a Flexible Spending Account (FSA). It is now beneficial to discuss specifically how Michelle can benefit from a FSA. Michelle can benefit from a FSA in the following ways:

- Michelle is in the 28% tax bracket.
    - → ***This means that every dollar she places into the FSA, she earns her an immediate tax break!!!***

---

[20] Under current law, an individual cannot begin to itemize their medical expenses until it reaches the threshold of 10% of their adjusted gross income.

- In the past, Michelle was not able to itemize her medical expenses since her medical expense fell shy of the 10% IRS Threshold.
    - → *With an FSA Account, she can lower her Adjusted Gross Income (AGI) and possibly qualify to itemize more of her expenses.*

- Due to the mechanics of how pre-tax accounts work, Michelle can increase her take home pay further!
    - → *She immediately puts more money in her pocket AND gets the benefit of purchasing the same medical items she would have purchases prior to having a FSA!*

In this section, we have attempted to demonstrate how individuals at the different points in their life and career can use the FSA to provide for themselves and their families. The benefit of using FSAs in this manner is that it is flexible enough to be used by people just starting out in life to people approaching retirement! As you will see later in this guide (See Appendix A), there are a number of uncommon items that an individual or family could use to improve their quality of life.

Tax Implications of FSAs

Written by James Fleming

Throughout this book we've discussed in various ways that your FSA reduces your taxes and increases your spendable income. Unlike many of the other pre-tax deductions, the FSA is a triple threat – it is a pre-tax deduction; it is reimbursable and then more you earn, the more valuable the deduction.

Let me explain – the U.S. Tax system is a graduated tax system which means the higher your income, the higher your taxes. There are 7 tax brackets. Therefore, all pre-tax deductions can reduce your taxable income and increase your take home pay.

Bracket	Tax Savings	Reimbursement and Tax Savings
10	500.00	5500.00
15	750.00	5750.00
25	1250.00	6250.00
28	1400.00	6400.00
33	1650.00	6650.00
35	1750.00	6750.00
39.60	1980.00	6980.00

Table 1 – Assumes both spouses take the $2,500 FSA Deduction for a total of $5,000

Let's take a look at the 25% Tax Bracket. You're looking at receiving, between your tax savings and your reimbursement, as much as $6,250.00. This is money you can now choose to spend or invest in any way you want.

This is like getting a tax free bonus or a sizable raise on your job all because you took advantage of a tax benefit that most people overlook.

Suppose you haven't saved for your child's college education and he/she is in the 10th grade. You could save the $6,250 for the next 3 years and contribute as much as $18,750 for your child's college tuition. Even better, because of the existing education tax credits, you could get an additional tax credit as high as $2,500 per year for 4 years, thereby putting $10,000 back into your pocket. This is a big win that rarely happens for individuals in the tax code.

So as we have been saying throughout this e-book, you have the opportunity to invest in stocks, bonds, real estate, pay off debt or college tuitions and student loans by wisely using the FSA. This is one tax law that the Congress and the Internal Revenue got right!

How to Use FSAs in Unconventional Ways to Generate Massive Benefits

Most of the information in this guide was very detailed and let's be honest, some of it was quite boring! My goal in going through this information was not to bore you, but a certain understanding of how the Flexible Spending Account works is necessary to appreciate why you should participate. Now that the necessary particulars have been dealt with, it is now time to discuss how you can use your FSA in ways that the IRS has not thought about (which are legal by way) to enhance your family's financial security.

Keep in mind that the information that I am going to share with you is somewhat complex. Every effort will be made, as has been the approach throughout this guide, to simplify the information as much as possible. Most of the approaches I am dealing detailing come from applications of my graduate work in systems engineering (namely inventory models if anyone is interested). Don't worry there are no formulas. Just know that there exists a firm mathematical basis for what I'm going to share.

Refresher on the 3 Benefits of FSAs

The benefits of Flexible Spending Account (FSA) are numerous and have been emphasized throughout this e-book. The reason for reiterating them in this space, is that these benefits are absolutely essential to how the average American can leverage this information to create financial security for themselves and their families. The primary ways that Flexible Spending Accounts add value to individual is through three (3) pathways. These include:

- An immediate tax break from the time when an employee signs up and funds are deducted from their checks on a pre-tax basis.
    - → This benefit is key to everyone, especially those employees at the top of the income distribution. Tax breaks for the average American are hard come by. FSA provide workers with an immediate tax break!!! *THIS LOWERS TAXES AND MAKES IT MORE LIKELY THAT AN INDIVIDUAL WILL GET A REFUND AT THE END OF THE YEAR!!!*

- The other major perk of the Flexible Spending Account (FSA) is that it provides a way for the average American to get a tax break on things they were going to purchase anyway!!!
    - → The benefit of this is that there is no change in behavior required to maximize your benefit. If you are sick, or need eyeglasses, or need to go to a specialist, you were going to go regardless of whether the Federal Government incentivized you to do so. ***THIS MEANS YOU GET THE BENEFIT OF DOING SOMETHING YOU WERE GOING TO DO ANYWAY AND CREATE OPPORTUNITIES GET MORE VALUE FOR YOUR MONEY SINCE THAT MEDICAL GOOD OR SERVICE WAS PURCHASED WITH PRE-TAX DOLLARS!!!***

- The last benefit (and in my opinion, the most exciting), leverages the previous two benefits and adds the ability to divert income in tax advantaged ways. This ability is huge, since most, if not all, major corporations of the 18th, 19th, and 20th centuries all created and/or expanded in their respective areas using favorable tax treatment to grow and prosper in their respective markets.
    - → *Diverting income in tax advantages ways, allows compound interest to work and is the basis for all types of investment.*

Creation of an Emergency Fund

Most financial experts agree that one of the bedrock pillars of financial security is have an emergency fund to deal with life's issues. Most Americans, when surveyed, do not dispute the need for emergency savings to deal with issues as they arise. The major concern seems to be how to save money for an emergency fund, when life's major concerns seem so overwhelming. It seems difficult to pay the rent or mortgage, food, gas, and other expenses, to say nothing of saving for a child's college education or retirement.

The issue seems to be access to viable funding line that can be used to provide for a big expense when needed. When the author was several years out of graduate school, he was laid off during the great recession. While some of his colleagues were stressed out over losing their houses, the author (using the tools in this book) was able to pay approximately six months ($20,000.00) of living expenses until another job was able to come along.

The best way to ensure this money does not get spent, is to designate or get a bank account for the express purpose of saving the FSA reimbursement funds. Once you have designated this account, you should do the following:

- Sign up for direct deposit of your FSA funds
- Direct these FSA funds to be direct deposited into this account
- Come up with a set of circumstances of what constitutes an emergency (e.g. Car breaks down, Family emergency, Mortgage is behind, etc.)
    - → If you are married or have a same sex partner, consult and come to an agreement about what constitutes an emergency

These tasks should enable you to create a wonderful opportunity build a decent emergency fund. Remember that since the IRS requires that employers pre-fund Flexible Spending Accounts (FSA), if you leave your job prior to the end of the year, then you can sign up for an FSA at your next job. The old employer, by law, cannot come after you for the funds. **THIS MEANS THAT IT IS POSSIBLE TO LEAVE YOUR JOB DURING YEAR, GO TO ANOTHER EMPLOYER, AND SIGN UP FOR THEIR FSA AND GET ACCESS TO ANOTHER $2,500.00.** This could greatly accelerate your efforts to build an emergency fund.

Use of FSA funds to contribute to Certificates of Deposit (CD)

Since FSA funds can be used in any fashion a person sees fit, it seems appropriate to discuss the concepts of how Certificates of Deposit (CD) work and how they may be used as a tool to create financial security for yourself and your family.

A Certificate of Deposit is a financial instrument, whereby an individual loans a sum of money (normally in the amount of $1,000) to the bank or financial institution for a set period of time. Since the bank has access to the deposit for a longer period of time and pays a higher level of interest, generally speaking, there are penalties for withdrawing money prior to the CD's maturity.

CDs are a perfect tool for building financial security. First, the penalty for early withdrawals tends to discourage people from withdrawing the money for frivolous reasons. This means that the funds grow and compound till maturity. Second, since CD provide a higher level of interest they can very easily be used to establish what is known as a CD Ladder.

A CD Ladder contains a number CDs of different maturities (maturities refer to the time period when a bank has to return the original money borrowed and the interest the CD generated). It is possible to purchase several CDs with maturities that come due every six (6) months. This means that if you, needed some money during a period when one of your CDs was coming due, you could withdraw the money from the CD Ladder and still have your other money working for you.

Creation of Vacation Accounts

The medical costs associated with stress are well documented. Perhaps some of those costs, were the reason for some of those medical expenses in the first place. With the hectic, high stress jobs worked by most people, it is even more essential that individuals take the time to refresh themselves.

The primary reason that most individuals do not get away is not desire, but rather cost. Most American's work in highly stressful jobs and do not earn enough to save. Using the information in this e-book can go a long way toward freeing up enough cash to take a long vacation or to take a series of local excursions. Now let's discuss how to make it happen!!!

Throughout this e-book, there has been an emphasis on using Flexible Spending Accounts (FSA) in ways that allow individuals to get reimbursed for medical goods and services they were going to purchase anyway. This emphasis on the importance of reimbursement is vital, however there is a need to explain how to leverage this information to in order to store funds for a vacation account.

The steps needed to accumulate funds for a vacation are as follows:

- Identify items that would normally be available for reimbursement from your FSA
    - → For items that you are not 100% sure about, it is best to:
        - Call the FSA Administrator and inquire about the item.
        - Check the Summary Plan Description (SPD). This is normally located on the FSA Administrator's website.

- Submit receipts to the FSA Administrator, along with the required forms. The FSA Administrator will provide forms to your either via email or mail.
- Establish a separate bank account for the purposes of depositing FSA reimbursements.
    → Some people prefer to have FSA reimbursements mailed to their home. The purpose of a separate bank account is to ensure that FSA funds do not get mingled into your personal bank account.

- Figure out where you would like to go.

Creation of Investment Accounts

Note: The information and recommendations contained within the next sections refers to financial information that the author has implemented in his personal finances and believes to be of value to the everyday American. The author is not and has not received any licenses to render financial advice. Individuals should seek out the advice of competent professions in the legal, tax and financial professions to apply the knowledge to their particular situations. Precise Innovations, LLC has established a partnership with Fleming Financial Solutions to help individuals who desire to assistance in implementing the information in this guide. Fleming Financial Solutions can be located at www.flemingfinancialsolutions.com.

I will admit that this is one of my favorite uses of Flexible Spending Accounts (FSA). FSAs can assist any number of individuals to free up resources to invest for themselves and their families' future. Using FSA funds to invest for future provides a number of opportunities. These opportunities, properly leveraged, can assist you with investing for the future, but moreover they provide the capital needed to fund home purchases, pay off credit card debt, or provide a way (through the tax code) to use your money to purchase cars, boats, etc. and have your account balances still rise. **Check back on the FSA website, www.fsamyway.com for additional information on webinars/seminars/speaking engagements for more details...**

Using FSA to fund Individual Retirement Accounts (IRA)

Individual Retirement Accounts (IRA) are some of the easiest investments for individual's to have. IRAs are really baskets (i.e. they can hold a wide assortment of investments) that can purchase assets, which can be used to fund an individual's retirement. IRAs are offered by many financial institutions, including some that operate only on the Internet. They have the following features that make them ideal:

- **Low Cost** – An example of a low cost IRA is offered through the Vanguard Group. You can purchase stocks, bonds, mutual funds, and other types of securities such as gold as well. If you **agree** to have your paperwork delivered electronically, they will waive the $20.00 annual fee. Go to www.vanguard.com for details.
- **Can hold various types of investments** – One of the individuals the author used to work with, used his IRA to purchase a rental property. The rent payments made by tenants were collected and reinvested back into the IRA, which could then be used to purchase additional assets. There are a number of rules and regulations associated with using your IRA to purchase real estate. Please engage with the appropriate professionals to discuss your options. Go to the website www.questira.com for more information.
- **Can lower taxable income** – The IRS states that, under certain conditions and subject to certain income limits, an individual can deduct up to $5,500 per year from their personal income taxes for contributions to their Individual Retirement Account (IRA) in some instances. Check with a Financial Advisor or a representative from your bank to learn more.
- **Are protected from creditors** – While no one want to think about the possibility of going into bankruptcy or being sued, the simple truth of the matter is that if an individual is sued, the Supreme Court has ruled that retirement savings held in IRA **CANNOT** be liquidated to pay off creditors.

For the average American, these benefits are quite substantial!!! Most everyday Americans do not have access to estate planning, corporate veils and other tools used by the upper class to protect their assets. Access to the tools of the rich, allows the average American to experience the financial security that the rich have known since the founding of this country. The rich have leveraged the financial tools mentioned above to shelter their resources from lawsuits, creditors and even the government! ***Now YOU can too!!!***

Using FSAs to fund DRIPS

FSAs can provide a number of benefits with respect to investing. Two of the most powerful tools for generating financial security are: Money compounded over a sufficient amount of time and Time. One of the largest concerns facing the senior managers of large corporations, is ensuring that the stock ownership of the corporation does not fall in hostile hands. To some degree this concern is self-centered (i.e. they want to ensure their own jobs). To ensure that individuals who would be favorable to interests of the corporation kept the stock, corporations adopted Dividend Reinvestment Plans (DRIPS).

DRIPS function a lot like 401k plans, in that the funds an individual places in the account is used to purchase shares of a stock. What this means is that individual sends money into the account which is used by the account to purchases the stock. If the price of a share of Microsoft stock is $40.00 per share and the account has $80.00, the account will purchase 2 shares of Microsoft stock. The shares are purchased on a regular basis, so if the price dips to say $38.00 the account will own a larger amount of shares[21].

There are several benefits associated with owning DRIPS. One of the primary benefits is that for every stock you own, entitles you to a cash payment called a dividend. Once a company declares a dividend, the money can either be sent to you as a check[22] or it can be used to purchase more shares of stock. If an individual keeps the stock and its associated dividends compounding long enough (e.g. 10 years), it can become a source of retirement savings or a way to send a child to college.

---

[21] This is also known as Dollar Cost Averaging. It is also how 401k plans work to increase values in specific funds.

[22] If dividend payments are sent to you, you will owe taxes on the dividends.

Another key benefit of DRIPS is the ability to attend shareholder meetings. Most people would ask why that would be a benefit. The answer lies in the IRS Rules and Regulations about stock ownership. The IRS allows individuals who own at least 1 share of stock of a corporation to write off the cost of attending the annual shareholder meeting. This means that if an individual is savvy enough to attend a shareholder meeting and combine it with a vacation or even a medical visit then that person could write off the trip and potentially itemize the medical expense. This of course depends on the particulars of their situation.

As an illustration, the author owns stock in Exxon Mobile Corporation. When their shareholder meeting occurred in Texas, the author flew in for the meeting, had breakfast and lunch and attended the annual meeting. He was able to itemize (i.e. write off) the following expenses:

- Roundtrip Plane ticket
- Breakfast and Lunch
- Had a dinner meeting with a colleague to discuss a potential business deal (e.g. additional write off)
- Hotel expenses (due to the meeting with the business partner to discuss a potential deal)

The third benefit that DRIPS offer is the ability to have an investment compound over large periods of time, without have the government take taxes. Taxes are only due on a DRIP when dividend payments are taken by an individual as cash. If no dividend payments are taken, then the investment and the years of dividend payments grows!!! This growth allows very small amounts of money to grow to monumental sums.

The final benefit of DRIPS is both their low transaction cost and low amounts that can be contributed. Most people think that relatively large sums of money are required to invest in the stock market. When the author began investing in DRIPS, he was a recent college graduate making $35,000 per year. He would send in checks to the trust company that administered the DRIP in the amount $20.00. They invested the money for a period of 10 years and it was the seed money that was used to purchase his first residence. The low transaction cost of DRIPS makes them an ideal vehicle to ensure that money is not unnecessarily eaten up in fees. This means more money is working for YOU to ensure your financial security.

Conclusion

This e-book has covered quite a bit of material. The goal of this e-book was to present, in a simple, easy to understand format, information that could enable the average American to:

- Save up to 30% on their taxes
- Purchase items in a tax efficient manner
- Open up a new income stream

Each one of the previous mentioned benefit provides some benefit to the average American, however together these benefits allow the average American to keep more of what they make AND to use their FSAs in unconventional (but legal) ways. Some of the ways that FSAs can be used is to:

- Get a therapeutic massage
- Purchase a high quality mattress and box spring
- Purchase a yoga or gym membership

Each of the unconventional ways listed above pretty much unknown to individuals who sign up to Flexible Spending Accounts (FSA). These benefits are especially beneficial since they positively impact stress levels. Purchasing these items will enhance your health and make you more productive in both your work and personal life.

We at Precise Innovations, LLC have endeavored to produce an easy to understand guide that would allow the average person to make more informed choices regarding their Flexible Spending Account (FSA) so that they could open up an income stream, purchase things in a tax efficient manner and enhance their quality of life. As such, this e-book is only one of several e-products and services that are aimed at helping the average American to enhance their family's economic security. Some of the additional products and services related to Flexible Spending Accounts (FSAs) include:

- *E-learning modules* – These modules describe, in detail, the Flexible Spending Account (FSA) concept, and how to use this knowledge
    - → Provide tools, tips, and forms to get the most out of FSAs
    - → Provide information, tools, and best practices to place the individuals and their families in a better place financially
    - → Create opportunities to invest to leverage money in new ways (e.g. Real Estate, Internet Lending, etc.)

- *Monthly E-courses* - Once a month, a trained facilitator will offer a course on the benefits of the Flexible Spending Account (FSA) and how these benefits can improve their quality of life. This course will take participants though a four (4) week program where the FSA concept is explained and information about how to get the most from FSAs are provided. The opportunity to ask specific questions regarding individual situations will be offered. Additional resources will also be provided.
- *Individual Health Consulting* – Some of our clients have commented that they need to be able to purchase FSA items on short notice, such as when they un-expectantly lose their job. Another situation occurs where they desire to use their FSA in an unconventional way. In response to these situations, we offer consulting services to:
    - → Identify how you can take advantage of FSAs based on your situation;
    - → Create a customized listing of goods and services that **YOU** can use to enhance your quality of life;
    - → Refer you to a number of vendor and medical practitioners that may be able to see you on a short-term basis

Send an email indicating your interest to info@fsamyway.com.

- *Individual Financial Consulting* – One theme that has consistently arisen out of conversations with our clients, is their desire for a "trusted advisor". Someone with whom they use these new found funds in ways that enhance their financial security. To address those needs, we have established a partnership with Fleming Financial Solutions, to provide objective, clear, and understandable financial information that will aid you and your family in creating opportunities that will last generations. Contact James at Fleming Financial Solutions. http://flemingfinancialsolutions.com.

- **FSA Seminars** – We have had a number of client request in-person meetings with our staff to discuss Flexible Spending Accounts and to provide information in a judgment free atmosphere. To address this need, we have been conducting a number of FSA Seminars around the country to share some of the other cutting edge tools we cover in this e-book in a one to 2 hour format. Check out the website, www.Fsamyway.com for details.
- **FSA Teleconferences** - Even though Flexible Spending Accounts (FSA) have been around since the 1970s, there are quite a few individuals who have no idea about what FSAs are and how they can personally benefit from them. Our FSA Teleconferences offer an exceptional opportunity to hear about the concept of FSAs from a real live expert! These calls last approximately 45 minutes to 1 hour and aim to educate individuals about how FSAs can enhance the quality of your life. Check out the website, www.Fsamyway.com for details.
- **FSA Apps©** - The IRS requires that individuals who take advantage of Flexible Spending Accounts **MUST** maintain their documentation. At the current time, Precise Innovations, LLC is working on crafting a series of IPAD© and Android© apps that will allow you to store both the 3rd party FSA Administrator forms and the actual receipts and store both of these in the Cloud.

Appendices

In the following sections, we will share a variety of very valuable information regarding using the FSA to your maximum advantage. Some of the information in these appendences provides a fairly detailed view of how to use FSA in unconventional ways. It can be a bit overwhelming (e.g. some of the FSA Eligibility lists) but this was done to be as comprehensive as possible. I would suggest that you think of the information as a reference and use it to look up things as you may need them. For example, if you want to get massages reimbursed, you would go to a specific doctor (e.g. Primary care or Chiropractic) and request they issue a Letter of Medical Necessity for back pain or general stiffness.

Appendix A: Unconventional Items that can be purchased with Flexible Spending Accounts (FSA)

Note: Some of these items require a Letter of Medical Necessity (LMN). If you get a LMN, you should be able to use FSA funds to purchase these items. All of these are items that our clients have purchases with FSA funds. Be sure to check with your 3rd party FSA Administrator for details...

- Abortion
- Weight Loss pills
- Hot Stone Massages
- Facials
- Botox Treatments
- Prescription Sunglasses
- Mattress and Boxsprings
- Tanning Bed
- Gluten Free food (the IRS has VERY specific rules about this. You should check the requirements with your accountant or other financial professional)
- Seeing a Naturopath
- Exercise Equipment (e.g. Elliptical, Treadmill, etc.)
- Hot-Tub
- Gym/Yoga/Tai Chi Membership
- Mileage to and from the medical doctor/massage therapist/etc.
- Personal Trainer
- Nutritionist (typically requires a referral from a physician)
    - Once a referral is in place, any herbs prescribed by the nutritionist to treat a disease would be covered.
- Over the Counter Medications
- Hormone Therapy (e.g. Testosterone and Estrogen)

Appendix B: Best Practices for dealing with Flexible Spending Account (FSA) Administrators

Flexible Spending Account (FSA) Administrators are agents of the employer and are used to administer FSA plans at a specific company. The employees at a number of FSA Administrators differ in their level of sophistication and knowledge regarding what is and what is not permissible under IRS Rules and Regulations. Most of these individuals are working from a script and the approvals for your claims is handled by higher level personnel. This can work to your advantage!!! What follows is a listing of 5 Best Practices for dealing with FSA Administrators:

1) **Be prepared for a fight!**

    Issue: The IRS has ruled that employers must "pre-fund" FSAs and treat them like insurance. That is the reason that if an employee leaves funds in their FSA, the employer gets to keep those funds. For this reason, it is essential to know the system AND to have all of your "ducks in a row". Sometimes FSAs Administrators will claim that they did not receive your paperwork and receipts, particularly if you are being reimbursed at a rate quicker than they think you should be.

    Resolution: Always keep your original documentation!!! NEVER send original documentation in the mail. If you fax and/or email your documentation and it does not reach your intended destinations within three (3) days, call the FSA Administrator AND ask for the fax number to an individual. That tends to work well.

2) **Try to send in receipts as soon as possible**

    Issue: The author has advised his clients to send in documentation to the FSA Administrators as soon as possible. The reason for this is that FSA administrators are notorious for losing documentation, claiming that documentation cannot be read, or just coming with excuses for why they will not pay a claim. There are some monetary incentives (that I won't go into) for the reason to try to hold onto the money. Suffice it to say, the best course of action is to get the documentation into them as soon as possible.

Resolution: Send in your documentation as soon as possible. This gives you enough time to resend the documentation should the FSA Administrator claim they did not receive it. I don't have any definitive proof of this, but I have noticed that when I submit receipts or use my FSA DebitCard for expenses in a rapid manner (i.e. spend $500.00 in a single month), they then start to claim that claims were not received. The answer is to know the rules and keep your documentation. Send it in as soon as they claim can be filed. It protects you and gets your money working for YOU as soon as possible!!!

3) **Create a log of who you speak with when you have issues.**

   Issue: Inevitably, when you deal with FSA Administrators, they are going to tell inform of what the IRS Rules and Regulations state and what their specific policies are regarding reimbursement. The best way to deal with the FSA Administrators is to ask for their name, and if possible, their supervisor's name.

   Resolution: Always ask to speak with a person's whose name you have received. When you call the FSA Administrator's call center and ask for a specific person, the author's experience has been that the clerk gives you the benefit of the doubt. This is key since sometimes the clerk has to exercise discretion and this means that they can give you the "benefit of the doubt" when deciding whether some expense meets the IRS standard.

4) **Always keep your receipts ready for inspection.**

   Issue: The IRS requires that all individuals who participate in the Flexible Spending Account (FSA) program have their receipts ready for inspection in case of an audit.

   Resolution: In response to the numerous requests and needs of our clients, Precise Innovations, LLC is in the process of developing an app that will capture both the required FSA Administrator forms and the associated receipts using the camera capabilities on most smartphones to include Apple IPhone and Google Android operating system. The app with use the camera function of the phone, to capture an image of a form and receipt and then store those images in case the IRS requests to see those forms and receipts.

5) **Speak in a courteous manner with addressing FSA Administrators.**

Issue: The individuals who work for the FSA Administrators are lower skilled and are most likely under time pressure to address your concerns and move onto the next call.

Resolution: Addressing in a respectful tone provides them with a reason to hear your concerns. While they may still have to tell you No in some instances (due to the IRS Rules and Regulation), they do possess some discretion.

Appendix C: List of Qualifying Events

Throughout this guide, there has been mention of the fact that FSAs are wonderful tools for individuals to save, invest and generally improve their quality of life. While using FSAs provide a number of benefits, the questions that our clients often ask is, "When can I sign up?" The answer that to that question is not as straight forward. The IRS has specified that individuals can sign up for FSA during certain periods of time. This period of time are called "Open Enrollment". Time periods for open enrollment differ by organization, but they are normally during October and November of each year. Once FSA participants sign up, then their choices for the next year (also called their annual election) are implemented. Funds are available on January 1st of the next year.

There are certain times and circumstances that allow individuals to sign up for Flexible Spending Accounts (FSA) outside of Open Enrollment. These times are either when the 1 of the following events occurs:

1) A person joins a new organization. After a person joins a new organization, there is a window of 30 days for them to elect to participate in the organization's FSA; OR
2) An person experiences a qualifying event

A Qualifying event is an event that signifies that something significant has occurred in the life of an FSA participant. Listed below are examples of Qualifying Events organized by whether an FSA participant increases their election or decreases their election:

- Increase Medical FSA election:
    → Marriage
    → Birth or adoption of child
    → Child who gains dependent status

- Decrease Medical FSA election:
    → Divorce
    → Child no longer qualifies as a dependent
    → Dependent dies

- Increase or Decrease Medical FSA election:
If your spouse or dependent:
    → Starts or ends a job
    → Increases or decreases work hours
    → Gain or lose eligibility for employer sponsored health insurance or health flexible spending coverage
    → Court order requiring you or another person to provide health coverage for an eligible child
    → If you, your spouse, or dependent gain or lose
    → Medicare or Medicaid coverage
    → Going on or returning from FMLA leave as allowed by FMLA requirements and Plan Rules

About the Author

Marion Williams

When clients in both public and private sector require an individual to analyze software systems, design strategies to minimize technological and project risk and explain complex information in a succinct manner, they turn to Marion Williams. Marion brings impressive credentials and experience to the engagements he has led. His experience includes advising senior-level government officials, military officers and C-suite executives for the past thirteen years.

Mr. Williams' extensive background in systems engineering, enterprise architecture, and information system strategy development, has provided him with the tools and techniques to address complexity in organizations. These tools and techniques have provided him with the unique insight to peer into the complex nature of the United States tax code. Mr. Williams uses this insight to create opportunities for both individuals and businesses to improve the quality of their lives and business' respectively.

As the managing director of Precise Innovations, LLC, Mr. Williams offers his client base the ability to address a wide range of challenges. The primary asset of his firm is to act as a "trusted-advisor" to their clients. Our flexible spending account suite of products and services teach how to access the access a tax-free income stream, create substantial tax benefits, and leverage funds into wealth generating assets that will last generations.

Precise Innovations, LLC is a full service management and technology firm that leverages the technology to create opportunities to enhance people's lives. These value added products and services aim to improve an individual's ability to lead a productive, enjoyable life and allow businesses to engage and serve their clients more effectively. To accomplish these goals, Precise Innovations, LLC creates a number of e-learning materials, e-books, seminars, white papers that aim to educate, inform, and help our clients meet their most pressing challenges.

To learn more information about Marion Williams and Precise Innovations, LLC please visit: www.FSAmyway.com

www.ingramcontent.com/pod-product-compliance
Lightning Source LLC
Chambersburg PA
CBHW021039180526
45163CB00005B/2201